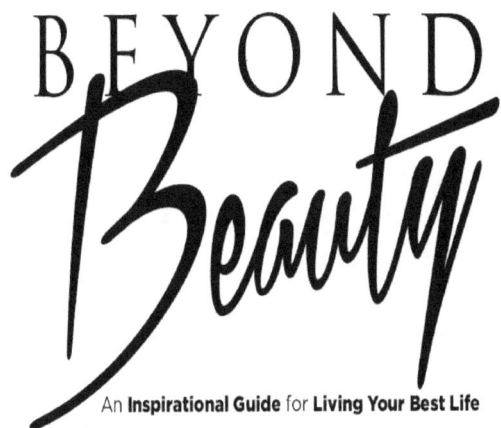

An **Inspirational Guide** for **Living Your Best Life**

Lakeesha R. Clark

Clark Creative Publishing

CANYON COUNTRY, CALIFORNIA

Beyond Beauty by Lakeesha R. Clark
ISBN 978-0-692-56125-6
Published by Clark Creative Publishing
P.O. Box 1152
Canyon Country, CA 91386

Copyright © 2015 by Lakeesha R.Clark
All Rights Reserved. This book or any parts thereof may not be reproduced, stored in a retrieval system, or transmitted in any form or by any means – electronic, mechanical, digital, photocopy, recording, or otherwise – without prior written permission of the publisher.

Scripture quotations marked (KJV) are taken from the King James Version of the Bible.

Scripture quotations marked (AMP) are taken from the Amplified® Bible, Copyright © 2015 by The Lockman Foundation Used by permission." (www.Lockman.org)

Dedication

I want to dedicate this book to the memory of my grandmother, the late Lula M. Johnson. She was the epitome of a virtuous woman of God. Her loving nature was present with everyone she encountered. She taught me the true meaning of unconditional love and faithfulness.

Granny, I love you!

Acknowledgment

I would like to thank everyone who has supported me along my journey thus far. To my mother, Bernetta A. Johnson, DMin., and father, John E. Clark, what can I say but thank you and I love you, I don't know where I would be without both of you! To the rest of my family and friends, your support and insight throughout the years has meant everything. I appreciate and thank you! To my Editor, Dr. Ebony Wilkins, thank you for helping me make this book a reality. You are the best! To Jason Caston, Internet Church Specialist, watching you go after your dreams had a significant impact on me and inspired me to do the same. Thank you! To my Graphic Designer, Cory Broussard, your work is amazing. Thank you for blessing my book with your skills! To the pastors whose ministries have been a blessing to me throughout my life, Bishop T.D. Jakes, Pastor Nisaac Rosario, Bishop Calvin Scott, Pastor Henry Coles, and Pastor Gilbert Burns thank you for preaching the uncompromising word of God.

To my heavenly father, there is no me, without you. Thank you for giving me the wisdom and strength to write this book. You gave me this idea many years ago and despite putting it off for so long, here it is. You are faithful to complete what you started in me. I love you, Lord!

Contents

Introduction..7

Chapter 1 Being You......................................9

Chapter 2 Esteeming Yourself..........................21

Chapter 3 Finding Purpose.............................35

Chapter 4 Saying Yes....................................47

Chapter 5 Developing Perseverance..................56

Chapter 6 Building Relationships......................68

Chapter 7 Financial Responsibility....................81

Chapter 8 Community Service.........................93

Chapter 9 Travel...102

Chapter 10 Beauty by Design.........................119

Bonus…Beauty Product Tips..........................124

Introduction

Beyond Beauty means looking past the outer person and uncovering the inner person, the true beauty God designed you to be. Go beyond the surface to see yourself through God's eyes. You were created for so much more. You are destined for greatness!

This book was written as a direct result of my life experiences and acknowledges some of the stages you go through as a young woman and how to overcome them and live victoriously through Jesus Christ. This book touches on many aspects of a young adult's life, such as purpose, self-esteem, confidence, career, travel, relationships, finances, and a relationship with

God.

You may be asking, what is my purpose? How can I overcome low self-esteem and build my confidence? How do I navigate relationships? How can I help my community? How can I start a budget? How can I persevere through any obstacle? I want to know God, how can I be saved? It is my hope that this book serves as a guide and resource that will help answer these questions, and give you a positive perspective on life. The foundation of this book is the Bible, which is the only standard of truth. This book will encourage and inspire you. As you read this book, do so with an open heart, to receive all that God has for you.

1

Being You

Be bold and courageous, what do you have to lose?

Beyond Beauty

Every girl has something special that makes her unique. God created you with specific gifts and talents that will enhance your life. You may be able to play the piano, sing, dance, or be a great listener for your friends. No matter how insignificant you think your gifts are they are great for the kingdom of God. Think about all of the things that make you different from everyone you know and recognize that those attributes are beautiful and contribute to who you are and the magnificent things you will do in the future. So embrace all of you, the things you like about yourself and the things you want to change, the sooner you do this the better you will be.

It took me a long time to embrace myself. Growing up I had always been the "odd" girl, or so I thought. I always believed that I was cute and had a great personality. However, I had always been overweight – the only one from my other siblings. I was also told I had a squeaky voice and that I was knock-kneed - which means I couldn't place my feet together effortlessly, and I wore glasses. Everyone always had an opinion of me; I was teased by many. I used to say, I just want to be "normal," but then I thought about it. What exactly is normal? Merriam Webster's dictionary gives many meanings for normal but for this purpose, normal is described as being "of, relating to, or characterized by average intelligence or development" and then I thought, no I don't want to be normal. I want to be an extraordinary person, someone whose life is not average, but truly significant and blessed beyond measure by God. I was also reminded that God set me apart so I will never be like anyone else. Why would I want to be? I am amazing, just the way God made me. You are as well.

There is no such thing as a normal person, because everyone is unique. So, I realized all of the things that were different about me were significant to the person I am. Because I am made in the image of God, the "oddness" was okay, and the only thing that mattered is what God said about me, which is, I am fearfully and wonderfully made in his image and I am the apple of his eye. With that being said, just be you. Your personality, your ideas, your intellect, and your beauty are what make you different from everyone else, which is a great thing. You are one of a kind, an original piece of art. You cannot be duplicated. No one else is exactly like you and no one else can fulfill the destiny God placed inside of you.

Acknowledge yourself, use your intuition, and pave your path for greatness. Be present with yourself daily by meditating on God's word. You may say, how can I do this? Before school or work have some alone time and pray whatever is in your heart to God. Express gratitude for your life, and use a daily devotional, which gives scripture for that day and keep the scripture at the forefront of your mind. God has many promises for you, one in particular to recognize and accept is James 1:5 (KJV) "If any of you lack wisdom, let him ask of God, that giveth to all men liberally, and upbraideth not; and it shall be given him."

Trust and use your intuition to help guide some choices. Using your intuition is making decisions based on your instinct. It cannot be explained by reasoning. You just have a knowing inside. Do not dismiss this knowing when making a decision, it is there to help you. The Holy Spirit is also your comforter and helps guide your choices. The Holy Spirit is God's spirit living in you. Galatians 5:16 (KJV) says, "This I say then, Walk in the Spirit, and ye shall not fulfill the lust of the flesh." In making important life choices I would pray and ask the Holy Spirit to give me guidance and ask for a peace regarding the decision. This way, your intuition and spirit will be aligned and at peace. Never make a decision if you don't have peace inside your heart regarding it.

I've mentioned Being You, which means using the unique qualities that God has given you. This may not come easy if you are void of God. If you are not a believer in Jesus Christ, I want to extend an invitation to you to pray the prayer at the end of the chapter and believe it in your heart and you will be saved. Your next step is to find and join a local Bible-based church that will teach you the word of God and get involved in a helps ministry at the church. Volunteering in the church will help you while you help others. Surround yourself with like-minded friends who can uplift and walk this new life with you.

If you prayed the salvation prayer below and have accepted Jesus Christ into your life, I want to be the first person to say congratulations. Your life will never be the same. A decision to live for Jesus Christ is the best and most important decision you will ever make. He is your Savior, Master, Lord, Father, Friend, Comforter, Healer, Redeemer, Peace, Hope of Glory, Sanctification, Faith and Righteousness. You now live in abundance, full of all of the promises of God and everlasting life!

Prayer for Salvation

Heavenly Father, in the name of Jesus, I want to be saved and have everlasting life. I believe Romans 10:9 (KJV) "That if thou shalt confess with thy mouth the Lord Jesus, and shalt believe in thine heart that God hath raised him from the dead, thou shalt be saved." I repent, please forgive me of my sins. Come into my heart, renew my mind, fill me with your Holy Spirit, and change my life for your glory. I believe Jesus is the only way to God and salvation. I believe Jesus died for my sins and rose again on the third day for me. It says in John 3:16-17 (KJV) "For God so loved the world that he gave his only begotten Son, that whoever believeth in him should not perish, but have everlasting life. For God did not send His Son into the world to condemn the world, but that the world through Him might be saved." Thank you for your unconditional love, saving me and making me a new creation in you. In Jesus Name. Amen.

Questions to Answer

1. Describe what "Being You" looks like, including the pleasant and not so pleasant attributes?
2. How can you work on turning the unpleasant attributes around for the better?
3. What potential have you not tapped inside yourself that can be beneficial to your future?

Being You

Beyond Beauty

2

Esteeming Yourself

Know your value, if you don't who will

Self-esteem is powerful. As a young lady, your self-esteem, your attitude and value of yourself should be high. If it is not, don't worry, it can and will change if you think, believe, and say it will. Philippians 4:8-9 (KJV) "Finally, brethren, whatsoever things are true, whatsoever things are honest, whatsoever things are just, whatsoever things are pure, whatsoever things are lovely, whatsoever things are of good report; if there be any virtue, and if there be any praise, think on these things. Those things, which ye have both learned, and received, and heard, and seen in me, do: and the God of peace shall be with you."

Esteem thyself by speaking the word of God to yourself. Say to yourself the things God says about you. Deuteronomy 28:13 (KJV) "And the LORD shall make thee the head, and not the tail; and thou shalt be above only, and thou shalt not be beneath; if that thou hearken unto the commandments of the LORD thy God, which I command thee this day, to observe and to do them." Words bear fruit. So always be mindful of what you say, whether it is positive or negative. It's a great idea to think before you speak, your words are powerful. Luke 6:45 (KJV) "A good man out of the good treasure of his heart bringeth forth that which is good; and an evil man out of the evil treasure of his heart bringeth forth that which is evil: for of the abundance of the heart his mouth speaketh."

When you speak, you are shaping your life with intention. So always speak life, which means speaking positivity to your situation or circumstance. I encourage you to speak the scriptures below over your life daily as a reminder of who you are, even if you're not having such a good day. Don't let anyone make you feel discouraged or sad. Your esteem does not come from them so don't give them any power. Your esteem comes from God!

Quick Scriptures to Say:

I AM a Child of God – Galatians 3:26

I AM Chosen and of Royal Priesthood – 1 Peter 2:9

I AM Blessed and Highly Favored by God – Luke 1:28

I AM More than a Conqueror – Romans 8:37

Esteeming Yourself

I AM Loved Unconditionally – Romans 5:8

I AM Healed by Jesus Stripes – Isaiah 53:5

I AM Redeemed – Ephesians 1:7

I AM a Temple of the Holy Spirit – 1 Corinthians 6:19

I AM In This World, Not of It – John 17:16

I AM a Doer of the Word and Not a Hearer Only – James 1:22

I AM Not Afraid, for My God is With Me – Psalm 23:4

God Has Not Given Me the Spirit of Fear, but of Power, Love and a Sound Mind – 2 Timothy 1:7

I Was Created in the Image of God – Genesis 1:27

I Walk by Faith, Not by Sight – 2 Corinthians 5:7

I Lack Nothing, God Supplies All My Needs – Philippians 4:19

I Can Do All Things Through Christ who Strengthens Me – Philippians 4:13

I Have the Peace of God – Philippians 4:7

No Weapon Formed Against Me Shall Prosper – Isaiah 54:17

There is a popular song by Donald Lawrence and the Tri-City Singers, called "Encourage Yourself," which sums up the confidence level you should embrace. You cannot wait on someone to give you recognition, esteem, or encouragement. When you set your mind to do something, you must encourage yourself, work hard and block all negativity from peers, family and friends. There will be external forces trying to block and discourage your progress. So, you must work hard to prevent any distractions that could potentially take you off track from going forward with your goals. If you are constantly having experiences with people that are not giving you positive energy and are not on your team, which means they don't want to see you win in life, it is time to reevaluate that relationship, and decide if it is a mutually beneficial relationship, a relationship which adds or contributes to your life and theirs in a positive manner.

It is imperative to recognize who is speaking life, greatness, and positivity into your life. Keep these people in your life. They are adding value to you. Add value to your relationships whether it is with friends, co-workers, or family, you want this behavior to be reciprocated. To discover if you are in a mutually beneficial relationship, ask yourself are they adding to my life, what am I gaining from this relationship that will help with my growth as I move forward and then pose the same questions to yourself regarding them? If you can't come up with a positive answer, have a conversation with this person if you would like them to still be a part of your life. If you realize nothing good will come from this relationship, separate yourself from them. Who you surround yourself with affects your outcome, whether it is success or failure. As you reach for the sky and pursue excellence some people may not want to be your friend anymore or you may need to remove some people from your circle of friends. Take the next few words and hold on to them tight, you must protect Your Mind and Heart it's so important. Proverbs 4:23 (KJV) says, "Keep thy heart with all diligence; for out of it are the issues of life." So, guard your heart with all diligence, speak positivity only, and add value to your relationships by being a blessing to someone else.

Being a blessing to someone else is a selfless act that sets you apart from your peers. You want to be set apart, which means not following, but leading. While you are being set apart from negative influences you may feel alone, but God will never leave you alone. Deuteronomy 31:6 (KJV) "Be strong and of a good courage, fear not, nor be afraid of them: for the LORD thy God, he it is that doth go with thee;

he will not fail thee, nor forsake thee." If you are called to be a leader you will stand out from the crowd. A leader's position is not easy. They must be knowledgeable and make final decisions. Leaders take on the most risk but their reward is always much greater. Leaders must build strong teams around them that are more knowledgeable in the areas where they need guidance. You never want to be the smartest person on your team. Surround yourself with positive people that can impart wisdom into your life and help you reach your goals. Pray that God gives you direction, orders your steps, and connects you with the right people. Once you have direction, are diligent and are in God's will; your goals and dreams have no choice but to flourish and workout for your good. Romans 8:28 (KJV) "And we know that all things work together for good to them that love God, to them who are called according to his purpose."

Prayer for Encouragement and a Sound Mind

Heavenly Father in the name of Jesus, thank you for reminding me who I am in you. Thank you for my purpose and destiny. Give me the power to encourage myself and believe only what you say about me. Help me to stay focused with a sound mind. 2 Timothy 1:7 (KJV) "For God hath not given us the spirit of fear; but of power, and of love, and of a sound mind." Lord I thank you for power to stand and be victorious. I want to be lead by the Holy Spirit. Lead me into the right direction, show me which goal to pursue first and equip me with the tools to conquer it. In Jesus Name, Amen.

Questions to Answer

1. **Evaluate your thoughts towards yourself. Are they positive or negative? If they are negative, start to change them.**
2. **What activities can you do to esteem yourself?**
3. **What can you do to add value to your current relationships?**

Esteeming Yourself

Beyond Beauty

3

Finding Purpose

Walk in purpose and you will never be the same

Children are asked what would you like to be when you grow up and they say the jobs they have been told to admire or have seen to have influence like doctor, lawyer, singer, firefighter, policeman and so on. If you could be asked that question today would you have the same answer? Some of you may say yes and some may say no. No matter what you answered, God has given you purpose, the reason you exist, the innate ability you have, which is to be pursued and fulfilled. The thing you do naturally and the thing you would do for free, yes for free, the thing that makes your soul sing - that is your purpose! Your career choice should align. Why would you not build a career around the thing you enjoy doing most? For this reason you hear many people say, I don't work a day in my life because I enjoy what I do. If you are unsure of your purpose, pray the prayer at the end of the chapter and listen for an answer. Sometimes people pray for things and don't take the time to listen for an answer. If you don't receive the answer right then, be assured that it's coming, and may come through visions, other people, and or in the word of God. Remember the Holy Spirit is your guide and you will always have peace in your spirit when you have the right answer, and that's for anything or any situation.

If you seek your purpose now you will have a more fulfilling life. You will be clear and firm on many decisions in life if you decide to trust God, and move in his direction and will for your life. I have known since I was a teenager that I had the natural ability to do hairstyles. Styling hair is a gift that has been passed down from my grandmother. She was a licensed cosmetologist with a salon in her home. I would watch her and do my hair. So, in my senior year of high school I started cosmetology school. I attended high school during the day and cosmetology school at night. Instead of taking the summer off during the summer after high school graduation and before starting undergraduate school or working full-time, I continued cosmetology school. I had a goal in mind, and I pursued a cosmetology education and didn't let anyone stop me. I went on to undergraduate school and in the first summer, I completed cosmetology school. I became a licensed cosmetologist while in undergraduate school. Because I stayed ahead of the game, I was able to work as a hairstylist while pursuing my bachelor's degree. The skill has always been with me naturally and is continuously nurtured by education and work. Knowing that working in the beauty industry is within my purpose has been helpful to me and continues to fulfill me.

When I say "within your purpose" this denotes that your purpose is dimensional. I believe you have purpose in your family, career, your community and in ministry. Purpose in ministry does not mean you have to be a minister in the pulpit, however, the Bible states the great commission to believers in Mark 16:15 (KJV)

"And he said unto them, Go ye into all the world, and preach the gospel to every creature." You must spread the word of God and stand for Christ; whichever way God leads you to do this, it could be as simple as showing the love of God to someone in need. You never know what people may be going through and you could be the only light of God they encounter; just be mindful of this as you engage with others. If you need help finding your purpose in ministry, there are tools such as spiritual gifts assessments to help guide you. Lifeway.com has an assessment and other great information on spiritual gifts you can use; those tools are located in the articles section titled Spiritual Gifts Assessment Tools. After completing the assessment, you will have results that will give you insight into your purpose in ministry. For example, one of your natural given abilities could be "administration." A gift in administration will not only be beneficial in ministry but will help you in so many areas of life, such as career, volunteering, and so on.

Before you seek those tools, pray and ask God our creator in Jesus name to guide you, show you your purpose in family, career, community and ministry and give you opportunities to fulfill it. God may not give you all of your purpose (family, career, community, and ministry) at once. He may give it to you in pieces, in the right timing for each appointed thing. Once you have any portion of your purpose, it's a great idea to create a vision board. This vision board will be a visual conception of your purpose. Habakkuk 2:2 (AMP) "Then the LORD answered me and said, "Write the vision and engrave it plainly on [clay] tablets So that the one who reads it will run." To create the vision board, gather some magazines that you are interested in and would have images to reflect your career and ministry, what it entails and your family. I would advise using some old magazines around the house. If you don't have any magazines you may have to purchase them. Cut pictures and words that depict your life in the future. After you cut your items, paste or tape them to a poster board and display them in a place where you will see it every day, for example on your bedroom wall or closet door. The vision board will remind you everyday of your purpose. When you see it visually, it is planting a seed in your mind and you are assured it will happen but only with your actions and God's help. After you have completed the vision board and have direction from God on where to start, initiate the work towards fulfilling your purpose and watch your life be forever changed.

Prayer for Purpose

Heavenly Father, in the name of Jesus, I thank you for giving me purpose. It says in Jeremiah 29:11(AMP) "For I know the plans and thoughts that I have for you,' says the LORD, 'plans for peace and well-being and not for disaster to give you a future and a hope." Lord, show me my purpose, within my career, community, ministry, and family so that I can fulfill it. I thank you for guiding me and trust that you know what is best for me. Lord, give me strength as I pursue my purpose and the power to stand in it. In Jesus Name, Amen.

Questions to Answer

1. What is within your Purpose?
2. If you have taken an assessment to find out your inherent gifts, what are they, and how would you apply them towards your purpose?
3. What steps can you take to fulfill your purpose within your family, career, community, and ministry?

Finding Purpose

Beyond Beauty

4

Saying Yes

Surrender to change, it's inevitable

Yielding to God's will can be a challenge when there is always something that can entice you to do the opposite. If you are like me, you always want to be in control of what's happening in your life and you want to know why something is happening if it is not what you expected. I have realized over the years that God's will is the only perfect will for my life, and if it is not in his will, I don't want it. You are most fulfilled when you are doing the things God created you to do. For years, I chased a career I knew I didn't want at all because it was the safe traditional path I thought would get me quicker to my goal in owning a salon. While being unhappy with where I was living, I decided to trust God and made the decision to move to another state without knowing where I would stay or work. Once I yielded to His will, He made provision for me to live rent-free for three months and work full-time as a hairstylist. God gave me the opportunity to open a salon suite part time and work for a Christian Nonprofit Organization full-time. While working at the nonprofit organization, I was connected with some awesome people that inspired me and assisted in changing my perspective about my beauty business. It was there that I decided to embrace my gift fully in the beauty industry. God has also revealed to me greater things I will do in ministry because I yielded to his will in every area of my life. When you submit your life and will to God, it no longer belongs to you. However, you have a better life because God is truly the head of it. You were chosen for greatness. God loves you and created you to do his will. Ephesians 1:11 (AMP) "In Him also we have received an inheritance [a destiny—we were claimed by God as His own], having been predestined (chosen, appointed beforehand) according to the purpose of Him who works everything in agreement with the counsel and design of His will" So, while it is not always easy yielding to God's will in everything, you will find that your best life will unfold.

Yielding to God's will does not mean you are perfect; no one is perfect. It means you are not steering the ship; you have a guided direction that is not your own. When you make mistakes, it allows you to have knowledge and insight to share with others. If you are at the point of making important life changing decisions and are unsure, pray first, and let God lead you. If you still need assurance, seek wise counsel. Wise counsel is someone lead by God. That person could be a mentor, pastor, parent, etc. Engage with someone who has knowledge of that situation that can give you good, sound advice. When receiving this advice it is imperative to have great discernment to take the advice and leave what does not pertain to you. Discernment is being able to decipher what is true and false, right or wrong. Discernment is important in every area of your life. 1 Thessalonians 5:20-22 (AMP) "Do not scorn or reject gifts of prophecy or prophecies [spoken revelations—words of instruction or exhortation or warning]. But test all things carefully [so you can recognize what is good]. Hold firmly to that which is good. Abstain from every form of evil [withdraw and keep away from it]." So, make sure to use discernment in all situations so you can be in the will of God and know the right decisions to make.

Prayer for the Will of God

Heavenly Father, in the name of Jesus, I thank you for your will for my life. Lord, I only want to be in your will. Make your will, my will. Keep my direction on your path. Matthew 6:10 (KJV) "Thy kingdom come, Thy will be done in earth, as it is in heaven," and Psalm 119:133 (KJV) "Order my steps in thy word: and let not any iniquity have dominion over me." Allow me to discern what is your true and perfect will for me. I thank you for wisdom and peace. In Jesus Name, Amen.

Questions to Answer

1. **Have you given your will up for God's will?**
2. **Who can you identify as "wise counsel" and why? Be sure to seek out someone, this will definitely enrich your life.**
3. **Do you use discernment when making decisions in your daily life?**

_____

_____

_____

Beyond Beauty

Saying Yes

5

Developing

Perseverance

Never stop, have a fixed mind

and do it again and again and again

until the manifestation comes

Developing Perseverance

In order to never give up on your goals, dreams, and purpose you need strength from above. Things in life may try to deter you from staying on track and on the right path. Do not give in. Ask God for his help, strength, comfort and direction to keep your mind focused. Becoming a strong woman mentally takes work. Dealing with past issues and facing current issues, all while keeping your mental strength is not easy. You may have experienced rejection, depression, felt lost, been bullied, had suicidal thoughts or other negative experiences, all of which are not of God! The enemy wants you to be consumed with those emotions so you won't succeed, but God only wants great things for you – to succeed, prosper, and have an amazing future! John 10:10 (KJV)

"The thief cometh not, but for to steal, and to kill, and to destroy: I am come that they might have life, and that they might have it more abundantly." Psalm 33:11-12 (KJV) says, "The counsel of the LORD standeth for ever, the thoughts of his heart to all generations. Blessed is the nation whose God is the LORD; and the people whom he hath chosen for his own inheritance." You will overcome. You are a survivor, destined for greatness, and empowered to live victoriously!

I can say you will overcome because I have dealt with some of those same negative issues and have been able to deal with them and move forward. A wise woman, who just happens to be an ordained minister, counselor, and my mom, once told me how to start the process of dealing with those emotions. First, write down all of your feelings and experiences, and then write down ways to overcome those emotions. Then, pray over them, and cast your cares to God. Then shred the paper. Shredding the paper is a symbol of those issues going away. They don't magically disappear but with prayer they will. 1 Peter 5:7 (KJV) "Casting all your care upon him; for he careth for you."

This is where healing starts. Healing means to restore your health; mind, body, and spirit. Healing in every area of your life is freely given by God. Isaiah 53:4-5 (KJV) "Surely he hath borne our grief's, and carried our sorrows: yet we did esteem him stricken, smitten of God, and afflicted. But he was wounded for our transgressions, he was bruised for our iniquities: the chastisement of our peace was upon him; and with his stripes we are healed." The scriptures above tell you God has already provided healing for you. It is time for you to confess your healing, believe you are healed and accept your healing. Being whole gives a peace and freedom that encourages you to stay on track and be diligent with your goals and succeed.

Success is not just given. You must be unwavering in your thoughts and diligent in your actions to produce a successful outcome. Every extremely successful person will tell you that the process of reaching his or her status did not come easy and the process is not envied. It takes an action plan, hard work and a sold out mind, a mind that cannot be changed and faith to keep you on track when the process gets hard and things don't turn out how you first imagined. Try, try, and try again and again until the manifestation comes. Galatians 6:9 (AMP) "Let us not grow weary or become discouraged in doing good, for at the proper time we will reap, if we do not give in."

You may be wondering, what is an action plan? An action plan is exactly what it sounds like. It is a written plan that lists steps to take to fulfill a specific goal, with resources needed and a timeline that states when to complete each task, until the goal is reached.

You may use an action plan for many areas of your life; whether it is a personal or professional goal you want to achieve. The only way it will work is if you not only create the action plan, but also put it into action. Action is such an important part of your faith. James 2:17(KJV) "Even so faith, if it hath not works, is dead, being alone." So, I encourage you to put your goals into action with the plan God has given you.

God has a plan for all of us and it is better than we could imagine. We must trust him completely. Proverbs 3:5-6 (AMP) "Trust in and rely confidently on the LORD with all your heart and do not rely on your own insight or understanding. In all your ways know and acknowledge and recognize Him, And He will make your paths straight and smooth [removing obstacles that block your way]." In order to go after our goals it is imperative that our goals are in alignment with God's will and that we pray for direction, favor, and resources to fulfill its purpose from God. As you can already see from the previous chapters that prayer is the answer for everything; and it truly is. God created you so why not go to your creator in prayer for anything in your life. Jeremiah 29:12-13 (KJV) "Then shall ye call upon me, and ye shall go and pray unto me, and I will hearken unto you. And ye shall seek me, and find me, when ye shall search for me with all your heart." Open your heart to receive what God says and be obedient in doing what he says. You must have a grateful attitude and be a willing vessel, surrendering to God's will. After you pray, rejoice and believe you have the victory. 1Thessalonians 5:16-18(KJV) "Rejoice evermore. Pray without ceasing. In everything give thanks: for this is the will of God in Christ Jesus concerning you."

Prayer for Perseverance

Heavenly Father, in the name of Jesus, I thank you for filling me with purpose and showing me how to fulfill it. I am seeking you for guidance, direction, a strong mind and resources to reach my fullest potential. Thank you for giving me the drive and strength to overcome any obstacles and a spirit that will never ever give up. I will not be distracted by external forces. I will stay focused on the goal and it will prosper in Jesus Name, Amen.

Questions to Answer

1. What are your goals?

2. Are your goals aligned with God's will for your life?

3. What resources will you need to get started?

4. What is your action plan to help you avoid pitfalls in the process?

Beyond Beauty

Developing Perseverance

6

Building Relationships

Be intentional, loving others requires effort

Building Relationships

Despite the negative images of relationships on television, the songs that degrade women, and the unhealthy relationships you may see in school, your community or family, God has designed the way we as men and women should treat each other. Use his word as the basis for any relationship you may have. Love is the key, In Mark 12:30-31(KJV) God said, "And thou shalt love the Lord thy God with all thy heart, and with all thy soul, and with all thy mind, and with all thy strength: this is the first commandment. And the second is like, namely this, Thou shalt love thy neighbour as thyself. There is none other commandment greater than these." Treat others with respect and dignity. Luke 6:31(AMP) "Treat others the same way you want them to treat you." Always let your light shine, even in the midst of darkness. I know it may not always be easy to show God's love, especially to the "haters" that try to bring you down. Just remember they have no position in your life but to prove that you are doing great things and blessed by God. So don't feed the negativity they bring, ignore what they say, pray for them, and remind yourself who you are in God by speaking his word over your life.

God created us to be connected to one another, helping one another. You cannot make it in this world by yourself. You need other people to live this life following Jesus Christ. Connect with other Christians that you can rely and depend on for prayer and comfort as you navigate through life. As you connect with others never forget the importance of your family. The relationship between your families, particularly your parents, is to be held with great regard. Ephesians 6:1-3 (AMP) "Children, obey your parents in the Lord [that is, accept their guidance and discipline as His representatives], for this is right [for obedience teaches wisdom and self discipline]. Honor [esteem, value as precious] your father and your mother [and be respectful to them]—this is the first commandment with a promise— so that it may be well with you, and that you may have a long life on the earth." Whether they have played a significant role in your upbringing or you feel let down by them because they weren't there or treated you horribly, they are still the reason you exist, and your honor for them is not really for them, it is for you. Your first priority is to please God and by honoring them, you please Him and He will bless you. It may not be easy if you haven't had great relationships with them, but God can turn your heart around and give you fresh eyes in how you regard them. Forgive the past, have faith, and believe prayer changes everything.

You may be thinking forgiveness is easier said than done and you're right, but forgiveness will always be essential to you living well. Forgiveness is not for the person that has wronged you. It is for you. Harboring unforgiveness is not healthy. You will not be able to truly move forward if you have unforgiveness in your heart. I have been challenged in this area before so, I know well how imperative it is to forgive. I was able to forgive and overcome only with the help of Jesus Christ. So, pray and ask God to help you forgive and to change the way you feel about the person, and He will. It may not change overnight but with time and a heart to please God you will be victorious.

As you learn the art of forgiveness, it will become easier to do. So, have a forgiving heart so that God will forgive you. Mark 11:25-26 (AMP) "Whenever you stand praying, if you have anything against anyone, forgive him [drop the issue, let it go], so that your father who is in heaven will also forgive you your transgressions and wrongdoings [against Him and others]. ["But if you do not forgive, neither will your Father in heaven forgive your transgressions."] " Once you have made up your mind to walk in forgiveness there will be circumstances there to test you but don't give in, remembering your stance, forgiveness always. So, while in school or on the job, don't allow your mood to be dictated by someone else. Don't allow anyone or anything to anger or persuade you to say or do something unethical or out of character. Remember, you have a strong mind and can choose to live a life of positivity and blessings. Your mind is powerful and too important for you to be influenced negatively. Negative thoughts can turn into harmful actions that may get you off track, actions that are harmful to your mind, body, and soul.

Those actions are sin. Sin separates you from God. You may ask what is Sin? According, to 1 John 3:4 (AMP) "Everyone who practices sin also practices lawlessness; and sin is lawlessness [ignoring God's law by action or neglect or by tolerating wrongdoing—being unrestrained by His commands and His will]." If you have sinned, God is ever merciful and gracious to us that all He asks is for you to repent and live a life pleasing to Him. God does not expect us to be perfect. He knows we will stumble and fall sometimes, so He forgives us. Acts 3:19 (AMP) "So repent [change your inner self—your old way of thinking, regret past sins] and return [to God—seek His purpose for your life], so that your sins may be wiped away [blotted out, completely erased], so that times of refreshing may come from the presence of the Lord [restoring you like a cool wind on a hot day]" Trust God, live by his word and enjoy life.

You are a precious gift. Your value is far more than you can imagine. Proverbs 31:10 (AMP) "An excellent woman [one who is spiritual, capable, intelligent, and virtuous], who is he who can find her? Her value is more precious than jewels and her worth is far above rubies or pearls." You are perfect in God's eyes and his opinion is the only one that matters. No matter your size, weight, height, hair color, hair texture, skin color or race. You are God's perfect design and He built you the way He desired. Your unique qualities and characteristics are what make you who you are. There is not another person like you.

Prayer for God-Centered Relationships

Heavenly Father in the name of Jesus, thank you for being the example for my relationships. Lord, please surround me with people of wisdom and peace. Let my relationships be positive and uplifting with you at the center. Plant in me a heart of forgiveness. Give me Christian friendships that are fun, edify my spirit, and impact the community. Thank you for your unfailing love and grace in Jesus Name, Amen.

Questions to Answer

1. How can you show God's love in your relationships?
2. Evaluate your current relationships, are they positive or negative and why?
3. Are you easily persuaded by others? If so, what do you think causes this and how can you change it?

Building Relationships

Beyond Beauty

7

Financial Responsibility

Get an understanding, create structure, and improve your financial position

Being financially responsible is not taught in most high schools but it is imperative for a prosperous life. Financial responsibility is basically not living beyond your means and being consciously aware of how much you're spending and saving. First, you must have your financial priorities in order to be successful in that area. Success does not mean you are rich. Success means your needs are met, you have savings, and can live comfortably. A guide to prioritizing your finances is by tithing, giving offerings, paying yourself, saving, and investing. It is important to tithe first from your income; Proverbs 3:9 (KJV) "Honour the LORD with thy substance, and with the first fruits of all thine increase." You may wonder what to give for your tithes; it is 10% of your income. Genesis 28:22 (KJV) "And this stone, which I have set for a pillar, shall be God's house: and of all that thou shalt give me I will surely give the tenth unto thee."

God commands giving your tithes and offerings but your heart must be right while giving. Giving the tithe and offering is very beneficial, it creates financial blessing in your life and blocks curses from your finances. Malachi 3:10 (KJV) "Bring ye all the tithes into the storehouse, that there may be meat in mine house, and prove me now herewith, saith the LORD of hosts, if I will not open you the windows of heaven, and pour you out a blessing, that there shall not be room enough to receive it." Luke 6:38 (KJV) "Give, and it shall be given unto you; good measure, pressed down, and shaken together, and running over, shall men give into your bosom. For with the same measure that ye mete withal it shall be measured to you again." So, you now understand the importance of giving.

Giving is such a blessing, Jesus Christ gave the ultimate sacrifice for us; so when you give do it cheerfully, as it says in 2 Corinthians 9:6-7 (KJV) "But this I say, He which soweth sparingly shall reap also sparingly; and he which soweth bountifully shall reap also bountifully. Every man according as he purposeth in his heart, so let him give; not grudgingly, or of necessity: for God loveth a cheerful giver." When your finances are in order you can focus on other aspects of your life, being certain this is not a worry. Struggling financially is hard. So, mastering this area of life will only propel you to greater circumstances in the future.

Having money creates freedom and opportunities in life that you may not otherwise have. When you work, you don't do it for the money, you do it because you are purposed to do it. When you have this mindset you will be able to weather some of the challenges that come from working. There will always be challenges but you will face them head on and push past them by coming out victorious on the other side.

I created the chart on the next page to give you a visual of what being financially responsible and successful will look. If you need a constant reminder tear the next page out of the book and place this chart in your home.

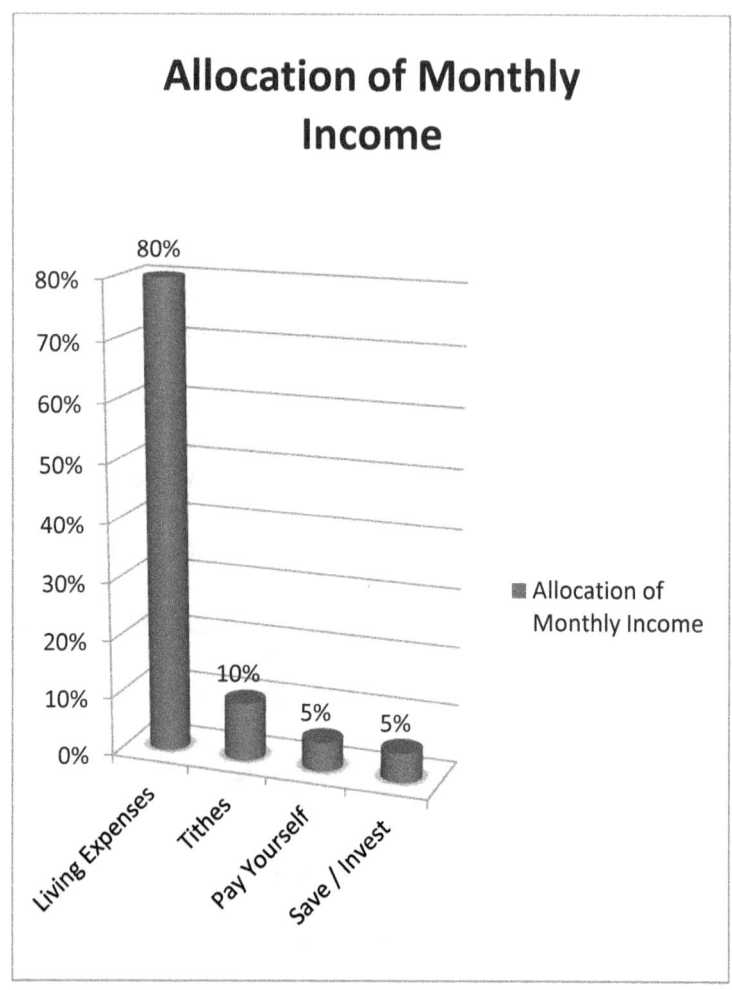

To help you get on the right track and manage your finances, I have created a budget chart on the next page for you to input and track your spending for one month. Usually you will get paid every two weeks so you can allocate the dates and bill items for your spending as you see fit, based on the bills you have accumulated.

Beyond Beauty

Date	Item/Bill Name	Amount	Notes
	Tithes		
	Rent		
	Groceries		
	Offering		
	Utilities		
	Offering		
	Cell phone		
	Car / Transportation		
	Groceries		
	Credit Card		
	Pay Yourself		
	Savings		
	Invest/Retirement		
	Shopping/Clothing etc		
Total Monthly Income			
Total Expenses			
Total Left Over			

Prayer for Being Financially Responsible and Prospering

Heavenly Father in the name of Jesus, thank you for being the ultimate giver. Lord, I want to be blessed in my finances not only for myself but to bless others. Lord, help me to make wise decisions with my money. Lord, I thank you that as I give according to your word, you will pour out to me a financial breakthrough. I thank you that as I sow my monetary seed, I will reap a harvest. I thank you that all my needs are met and I am living in abundance. In Jesus Name, Amen.

Questions to Answer

1. Do you live beyond your means? If so, in what areas can you make wiser financial decisions?

2. Do you give of your time and money?

3. How do you feel when you give to others, and why?

_____

_____

_____

_____

_____

Financial Responsibility

Beyond Beauty

8

Community Service

Welcome the chance to give to others; it will be exactly what you need

Your community is an essential part of your growth. It is important to understand this and to serve. Community is not just your hometown, it is also wherever you go - to college, work, church and live. You will find once you engage, build relationships and are of service to others, your life will become enriched in a great way. Hebrews 13:16 (KJV) "But to do good and to communicate forget not: for with such sacrifices God is well pleased." The list below is ideas of community service that can help you get started.

Volunteer Opportunities

Senior citizen homes

Homeless shelters

Food banks

Community Service

Salvation Army

After school programs for elementary and secondary students

Big Brothers & Big Sisters of America

Boys and Girls Scouts

Kids summer camps

Habitat for Humanity

Helps Ministry at your Church

Community gardens

And so on…..

To get involved with the listed suggestions, contact your local organizations.

Since high school I have been involved with community service projects. I worked with an abstinence program, homeless shelters, a help ministry at my church, community garden, an international NGO (non-governmental organization) in Switzerland, etc. So, I can attest to the beautiful gift you receive in helping others. Your life is not about you. Having a servant's heart and the mind of Christ will take you more places than you could have ever imagined. You may wonder how can I have the mind of Christ? You do this by renewing your mind with the word of God. Ephesians 4:23-24 (KJV) "And be renewed in the spirit of your mind; and that ye put on the new man, which after God is created in righteousness and true holiness."

Learning to be selfless is the key to life. Mark 8:35 (KJV) "For whosoever will save his life shall lose it; but whosoever shall lose his life for my sake and the gospel's, the same shall save it." Philippians 2:3-4 (KJV) "Let nothing be done through strife or vainglory; but in lowliness of mind let each esteem other better than themselves. Look not every man on his own things, but every man also on the things of others." Being selfless is being Christ-like. Although it may not be easy, try to maintain this as a staple in your life and die to your own selfish wants and surrender to God's will. It will soften your heart, make you more understanding, put things into perspective, and please God.

Prayer for a Servant's Heart and Opportunities to Serve

Heavenly Father in the name of Jesus, thank you for being the ultimate servant. Give me a renewed mind and a heart like yours to serve others. Show me opportunities to serve and bless someone else. Surround me with other like-minded individuals as I serve others. Thank you for loving and guiding me in Jesus Name, Amen.

Questions to Answer

1. **How can you use your skills and resources to help others often?**
2. **What community service activities will you participate in, and why?**

3. What does it mean to have a servant's heart?

Beyond Beauty

Community Service

9

Travel

Enhance your life by investing in travel

Travel

Experiencing God's creation through travel has been one of the best decisions I could have ever made. During my graduate program, I studied abroad in Europe. I was introduced to people from all over the world, different customs and viewpoints, foods, ways of living, languages, and beautiful architecture. I traveled to London, Switzerland, Italy and France. The beauty each place has to offer is unparallel to the next. London is somewhat fast-paced with many shops, beautiful architecture, great public transportation and is rich in history. Switzerland is more laid back with calming waters, the finest shops, and rooted in tradition; most retailers observe Sunday and close stores. Italy is beautiful with awesome food, shopping and culture. France has great museums, is very romantic, and is a shopper's paradise. Studying abroad changed my life. It was my first international encounter and I would not be the same without having committed myself to the experience. I recommend making a study abroad program mandatory as a part of your college experience. If you decide to get a trade or join the workforce, travel abroad as a vacation. You will be the better for it. Since my adventures abroad, I make it a priority to travel both nationally and internationally.

Traveling frees your mind and exposes your life skills. I traveled alone and while it was a somewhat intimidating feeling of the unknown, it worked for me because I was 25 years old, in college where I met many people and worked an internship. I wouldn't say you should travel abroad alone unless you are responsible, comfortable in your own skin, appreciate differences in people, and open to new experiences. Safety is first, so always be aware of your surroundings and stay in groups.

After traveling you will realize all of the possibilities life has to offer. If you ever felt stuck in your daily routine and need a refreshing embrace, travel and notice how your problems become small and your focus shifts. Your mind is expanded and you find commonalities and differences with others. Your commonalities bring you together and the differences show the unique qualities that each person needs in some way.

You are becoming a well rounded individual with insight, understanding, and appreciation for all people. Romans 15:7 (KJV) says, "Wherefore receive ye one another, as Christ also received us to the glory of God." Your inner beauty shines with acceptance of others.

Since you're on this journey and may decide to travel, I have listed some attractions, shopping destinations, and restaurants on the next few pages that you should try in a few well-known places in the world.

Travel

London, England

Restaurants

Nandos
113 Baker Street
London, United Kingdom
+44 20 3075 1044
www.nandos.co.uk

Baileys Fish and Chips
115 Dawes Road
London SW6 7DU
United Kingdom
+44 20 7385 2021
www.baileysfulham.com

Attractions

The Original Tour
+44 (0) 20 8877 1722
www.theoriginaltour.com

London Eye
London SE1 7PB, United Kingdom
+44 871 781 3000
www.londoneye.com

Shopping

Oxford Street and Regent Street– They both have great stores up and down the street for the fashionista in you!

www.oxfordstreet.co.uk
www.regentstreetonline.com

Paris, France

Restaurants

Eggs & Co
11 Rue Bernard Palissy
75006 Paris, France
+33 1 45 44 02 52
www.eggsandco.fr

Restaurant PDG
20 Rue de Ponthieu,
75008 Paris, France
+33 1 42 56 19 10
www.restaurantpdg.fr

Le Café de Mars
11 Rue Augereau,
75007 Paris ,France

Travel

+33 1 45 50 10 90
www.cafedemars.com

Attractions

Paris L'Open Bus Tour
13 Rue Auber
75009 Paris, France
+33 1 42 66 56 56
www.paris.opentour.com/en/

The Eiffel Tower
Champ de Mars
5 Avenue Anatole France
75007 Paris, France
+33 892 70 12 39
www.toureiffel.paris/en

The Louvre
75058 Paris – France
+33 (0)1 40 20 53 17
www.louvre.fr/en

Fragonard Parfumeur
Le musée du parfum
9 rue Scribe
75009 Paris, France
+33 (0) 1 47 42 04 56
www.fragonard.com

Shopping

Chic Shopping Paris
Book a shopping Tour!
15 rue de la Forge Royale,
75006 Paris, France
+33 9 77 19 77 85
www.chicshoppingparis.com

Beaugrenelle Paris
12, rue de Kinois
75015 Paris, France
+33 1 53 95 24 00
www.beaugrenelle-paris.com

Printemps
64, Boulevard Haussmann,
75009 Paris, France
www.departmentstoreparis.printenps.com

Geneva, Switzerland

Restaurants

Le Relais d'Entrecôte
6, Rue Pierre-Fatio
1204 Genève, Switzerland
+41 22 310 60 04

Travel

www.relaisentrecote.fr

Café du Centre
Place du Molard 5
1204 Genève, Switzerland
+41 22 311 85 86
www.cafeducentre.ch

Attractions

Swiss Boat Excursion
Quai du Mont-Blanc 4
1201 Genève, Switzerland
+41 (0)22 732 47 47
www.swissboat.com

Palais des Nations
1211 Genève, Switzerland
+41 22 917 12 34
www.unog.ch

Take the tour and visit the broken chair monument outside.

Patek Philippe Museum
Rue des Vieux-Grenadiers 7
1205 Genève, Switzerland
+41 22 807 09 10

www.patekmuseum.com

GoldenPass
Rue de la Gare 22 Case Postale 1426
1820 Montreux
+41 (0)21 989 81 90
www.goldenpass.ch/en

Experience attractions that are quick trips by train, especially to nearby cities Montreux and Gruyères.

Take the Golden Pass train tour package for the Train du chocolat (The Chocolate Train) and the Gruyères town and cheese demonstrations.

Shopping

Designer shops are on the streets between Rue du Rhône and Rue de Rive

Manor (a department store)
Rue Cornavin 6
1201 Genève Switzerland
+(0)22 909 46 99
www.manor.ch/fr/u/store/GEN

Venice, Italy

Restaurants

Pizzeria Trattoria all'anfora
Lista Vecchia dei Bari, 1223,
30135, Venice, Italy
+39 041 524 0325
www.pizzeriaallanfora.com

Osteria di Santa Marina
Castello,
Campo Santa Marina 5911
30122 Venice, Italy
+39 041 528 5239
www.osteriadisantamarina.com

Gelatoteca SuSo
Calle della Bissa, 5453,
30124 San Marco, Venice, Italy
+39 348 564 6545
www.gelatovenezia.it

Attractions

St. Mark's Basilica
San Marco, 328,
30124, Venice, Italy

+39 041 270 8311
www.basilicasanmarco.it

Venice Free Walking Tour
Campo SS. Apostoli,
30121 Venice, Italy
+39 392 987 0129
www.venicefreewakingtour.com

Book a Gondola ride
There are many websites to use to book a gondola ride; here are two of them below to check out.
www.viator.com
www.localvenicetours.com

Shopping

Raggio Veneziano
(For leather purses)
Campo Santo Stefano – San Marco 2953
30124 Venice, Italy
+39 041 241 2712
www.raggioveneziano.com

There are also many shops throughout Venice with unique jewelry and art.

Prayer for Travel

Heavenly Father, in the name of Jesus, I trust you know the plans for me. I would like to explore the earth you created. Please show me the best travel destinations I should visit and give me favor with all vendors. Give me the resources for the trips and connect me with the right people. I want to have great experiences and understand other cultures. Thank you for guidance and provision for the trips in Jesus Name, Amen.

Questions to Answer

1. **Where would you like to travel?**
2. **What will you need to plan to start your travel journey?**

3. Would you travel alone, or in a group, and why?

Travel

Beyond Beauty

10

Beauty by Design

Thrive in life with charisma, grace, and style

To design is to plan and make (something) for a specific use or purpose, according to Merriam Webster Dictionary. You have been designed by God with specific purpose. You will do greater things in life that you could not even imagine, if you believe. John 14:12-13 (KJV) "Verily, verily, I say unto you, He that believeth on me, the works that I do shall he do also; and greater works than these shall he do; because I go unto my Father. And whatsoever ye shall ask in my name, that will I do, that the Father may be glorified in the Son." It is my hope that you have clearly and completely defined your essential characteristics that make you the awesome person you are. I trust you have gained powerful, insightful information from this book that will call you to action. Trust God, keep him first, reach for and complete your goals with a plan. You are designed and defined for greatness. Never accept mediocre (in any area of your life), pursue your goals with focus and persistence. Again, block any naysayers and surround yourself with positive people only. Choose God's guidance in all decisions and watch his design for your life take form.

Remember you are God's chosen. Nothing can separate you from the love of God. Romans 8:38-39 (KJV) "For I am persuaded, that neither death, nor life, nor angels, nor principalities, nor powers, nor things present, nor things to come, Nor height, nor depth, nor any other creature, shall be able to separate us from the love of God, which is in Christ Jesus our Lord." Everything you need is in Jesus, so seek Him. I pray that your faith has been heightened and that you are transformed by the renewing of your mind. Romans 12:2 (KJV) "And be not conformed to this world: but be ye transformed by the renewing of your mind, that ye may prove what is that good, and acceptable, and perfect, will of God." It is my hope that transformation takes place and you and others start to see the emerging of a new woman, a woman who is more confident of who you are in God and yourself, a woman who is more determined to finish what you start and go get all that God has for you, a woman who is fearless in her approach to winning in life, a woman who is most importantly unashamed of the Gospel of

Jesus Christ, the giver of life, the answer to all questions, the Savior and Lord of all!

Bonus – Beauty Product Tips

Now that you have found, awaken or realized your inner beauty in God, I thought it would be great to share with you some of my go-to beauty products that will enhance your outer beauty so you will feel and look great. No matter the budget you have there is something for everyone. I hope you enjoy!

Beauty Brands for the Savvy Woman

(Low & High End Pricing)

For the Face

- Cleansers: Neutrogena & Clinique
- Moisturizers: Aveeno & Lancôme
- Face Mask: Freeman & The Body Shop

- Foundation: L'oreal True Match, Dermablend, & Mac Cosmetics
- Face Foundation Primer: Rimmel London & Laura Mercier
- Eye Shadow & Blush: NYX, Smashbox & Mac Cosmetics
- Eye Brow Kit: NYX & Anatasia
- Eye Pencil: COVERGIRL & Urban Decay
- Lip Liner, Lip sticks, Lip Gloss: There are so many to name and all of these usually go hand and hand so I'll give you a few to check out stila, NYX, Mac Cosmetics, Bare Minerals, Bobbi Brown and Origins

For the Hair

- The Pureology Brand –For all hair types and priced on the high end. I especially like the Perfect 4 Platinum Miracle Filler Treatment.

- The Aveda Brand – For all hair types, Aveda is in the medium range of price. I especially like the Aveda Brilliant Anti-Humectant Pomade for the edges of natural hair.
- The Pantene Brand - For all hair types and are priced on the low end.
- The Biolage Brand – For all hair types and is in the medium range for pricing.
- Shea Moisture Coconut & Hibiscus Curl Enhancing Smoothie – I had to add this product by itself. It's my favorite go to moisturizing product for natural hair and it's priced on the low end.

About the Author

Lakeesha R. Clark, MBA is an Author, Licensed Cosmetologist and Entrepreneur. Having been raised attending church her entire childhood she found that it wasn't until her freshman year in college that her relationship with God shifted to being her #1 priority. From experiencing disappointment, insecurity, and the twists and turns of life Lakeesha has overcome and is able to give you encouragement and inspire you! Lakeesha has a Bachelor's Degree in Business Administration – Emphasis Management and a Master's of Business Administration – Emphasis Marketing. She has a beauty business, *Natural Serenity Concepts*; a lifestyle platform for women. Lakeesha has been called to inspire and uplift women; whether it's enhancing your outer beauty or giving an empowering message!

For questions or to send in your testimony about how this book helped you email Lakeesha R. Clark at info@naturalserenityconcepts.com

To keep up with Lakeesha R. Clark visit naturalserenityconcepts.com